CONTENTS……

Introduction……………………….2

Baking Tools and ingredients…………………………….3

Baking a Sponge Cake Recipe……………………………..4

Method……………………………………………….5

Buttercream Recipe………………………………10

Covering the Cake …………………………14

Cover the cake with buttercream (A-B-C)

………………………15

Covering with Fondant (D)……….21

Decorating Ideas (E)……………………………26

Make a simple easy sugar craft bow……………….27

Make a simple easy shirt cake………………….28

Make a simple two tiers cake………………………………….29

Mistakes that makes your cake not perfect and how to solve them…………………………………………………….34

Video tutorials is available at " www.viodar-cakes.co.uk "

FIRST STEPS FOR HOME BAKERS

In this edition, we are going to start from step one. This is one of the most important steps to become a HOME BAKER. You will have enough knowledge to bake and decorate cakes whether you do it for special occasions, for someone you love or to become a professional Home Baker. All in simple steps.

I will teach you how to make delicious cakes, appealing to the eyes. You will learn an easy and delicious sponge cake recipe, a buttercream recipe for filling the cake, techniques and tips for covering the cakes with buttercream and fondant, as well as some simple decorations and designs for beginners, also a simple two tiers cake for intermediates.

This book tutorial has photos that show the step-by-step processes and final results to make sure you don't miss out anything! You will also have access to video tutorials to help you follow the book's instruction which is also suitable for people with hearing loss.

This book tutorial is for beginners and those who have been making cakes for quite a while but need to improve or correct techniques to bake more appealing and delicious cakes. Here, you will find anything you need to archive better results, attractive or delicious cakes.

I included a list of common mistakes, which can ruin your cakes, and how to correct them. So...... let's get started!!!

BAKING TOOLS

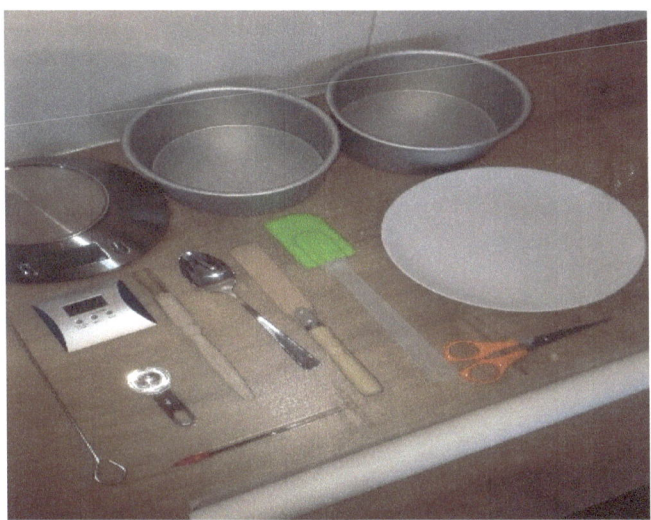

Metal spatula, plastic spatula, spoon, measuring spoon, metal cake tester, plate, pastry brush, timer, digital food scale, baking sheets paper, pen, scissor and two 6-inch baking pans-tins.

Mixer, mixing bowl, extra bowl, sieve and kitchen cloths.

BAKING A SPONGE CAKE

-Simple and Professional recipe

-Ingredients

-Baking

-Methods and techniques

Ingredients:

185g of Butter or Margarine (softened)

185g of Caster Sugar

4   eggs

1 tsp of Vanilla extract (or any other flavor)

185g of Self-raising Flour.

2 tsps. of Milk

Method:

1-Heat the oven to 180C/160C for fan assisted oven/350F/Gas 4.

2- Line two 6-inch cake tins with butter (just on the sides) and cover them with flour. Cut some baking paper in the shape of the bottom of the tin so that the cake does not stick to the tin whilst cooking.

3- Mix the buttercream and caster sugar until pale.

4- Add one egg at a time to the mixture and mix together.

5- Add the vanilla extract and mix.

6- Add self-raising flour and mix (sifted just before added).

7- Add the milk and mix until the mixture looks smooth.

8- Divide mixture equally into the two tins.

9- Put tins into oven for 20/25 minutes and check if the cakes are done. If they are not ready yet then leave them for 5 more minutes.

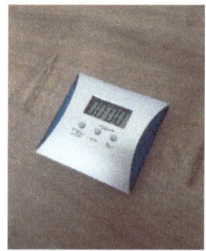 

10- Once cakes are cooked, leave them to cool down to room temperature (on top of a surface) but don't take them out of the tins yet.

Cakes must be at room temperature before being cut and filled.

Don't worry about cracks on the top as we are going to cut the top anyway.

Buttercream recipe

Ingredients: 250g of softened butter

500g of Icing sugar

1 tsp of vanilla extract

1 or 2 tsp of whole milk

Tools: Mixer, Flat beater, spatula, silicone spatula, spoon, measuring spoon, digital kitchen weighing scale, sieve and bowl and plate.

Method

1- Beat the butter in a large bowl until soft and a bit pale (by hand or mixer)

2- Add half of the icing sugar previously sifted on low speed and beat until smooth

3- Add the remaining icing sugar and beat on low speed not longer than 1 minute.

4- Add one tablespoon of the milk and Vanilla extract (or any other flavor) then beat the mixture until creamy and smooth. Start on low speed then medium, for no longer than 1 minute. For better results, use the silicone spatula to remove the butter on the sides of the bowl before mixing again. Now, mix on the high speed for 3-4 minutes in the mixer, add few minutes if you mix by hands.

5- Add more milk if necessary (to loosen the mixture).

If you wish, you could add any food coloring, just make sure it's mixed in well(spatula).

Covering the cake

A- Cut and fill the cake

B- Level the cake

C- Cover the cake with buttercream (2-3 times)

D- Cover it with Fondant

E- Simple decoration

TOOLS: A-B-C

HOW TO COVER THE CAKE WITH BUTTERCREAM

Video tutorial is available at " www.viodar-cakes.co.uk "

Method A-B-C

1- Carefully remove the cake from the mold and place it on a surface with the paper below it as the pictures show (once allowed to cool to room temperature).

2- With a very sharp knife cut the top to level it whilst also removing the dry parts of the cake. In this step, you could also use a ruler for precision. Repeat the process with the other one.

3- Put the base on top of the turntable, where the cake will be placed, and add a bit of buttercream with the spatula/palette knife to 'glue' one of the cakes down (remove the base paper first). IMPORTANT: turntable is not essential but it helps.

(check the tutorial photos for a clear guide in this step)

4- Add buttercream with a spatula to fill the cake and make sure it's leveled, don't worry if it goes off the edges.

5- Without removing the paper from the bottom of the other cake half, place it over upside down (with the part that has the paper at the top) and once it is in the correct place, flatten the buttercream all around the cake then remove the paper (see Photos as guide). Please note that if the cake is too soft it is recommended to avoid the removal of the paper from the top until the sides have been covered with buttercream. **Important:** It is essential that the cake is levelled so if you need to, use the tool shown in the third picture.

6- CRUMB COAT or first layer of buttercream: with the spatula spread more buttercream to the sides and then to the top covering all cake, then with the plastic spatula-edge side scraper, smooth and remove the excess as shown in the second photo. Please make sure you have removed the excess on the spatula each time so the excess of buttercream does not make marks/lines on it or remove buttercream when not wanted to.

7- Place the cake into the refrigerator-fridge for at least one hour until super firm and rigid. Keep in mind that if the cake is bigger, it will need more hours of cooling down to obtain the same result. If possible, I recommend leaving it overnight.

8- SECOND COAT: After an hour repeat the process one more time. In this step, you will feel that when removing the excess with the plastic spatula-scraper, the buttercream will join/sticks and cools quickly but at the same time is easier to apply because the cake is firmer. Then place it in the fridge again.

9- If necessary, repeat that step for a third time, leaving it in the refrigerator-fridge for at least 30 minutes. It is not recommended to leave the buttercream outside the refrigerator for more than 3 hours. Therefore, if the cake is larger then, after applying the first layer, put the remaining buttercream in the refrigerator and remove it approximately one hour before use, so it has time to get to room temperature. Once it reaches that temperature, you should beat/mix for a few minutes until looks as smooth as before. When you have applied the 2 or 3 layers of buttercream, leave it in the refrigerator/fridge at least an hour before applying fondant on it. It is important that the buttercream is not sticky and the cake is firm/hard.

(D) COVER THE CAKE WITH FONDANT

Video tutorial is available at " www.viodar-cakes.co.uk

Tools: 1-2 knives, a brush, 2 cake smoother paddle, a non-stick rolling pin(large), a spoon and turntable.

Materials: Fondant, corn flour, vegetable baking fat.

Before removing the cake from the refrigerator/fridge to apply the fondant, it is essential to have all the utensils and materials such as the fondant in the color of your choice on top of the surface in order to begin. Make sure your surface is clean and free of crumbs.

1- Remove the cake from the refrigerator/fridge. Apply with a brush some vegetable fat and cover the whole surface of the cake. Be careful not to add to much fat; this is only a step to glue the fondant to the cake and in case of mistakes (so you will be able to remove the fondant easily to start again). Possible mistakes: fondant is too small for the size of the cake, makes cracks or breaks. If any of this happens with the fondant this must be removed immediately, please do not continue putting it on.

The vegetable oil will help to avoid breaks on the cake or remove the buttercream previously applied

2- Dust the surface with corn flour to avoid the fondant sticking to the surface. If necessary add more. Knead the fondant for a couple of minutes to soften and make it circular (if the cake is circular). To roll it out to fit the cake, stretch the fondant with the roll just a little and rotate the fondant every time we stretch it. In low temperature, pass the hand around the fondant before you stretch it to warm it up, so it won't crack and will be more flexible and easier to stretch. Repeat this until it becomes a circle that is as even as possible and slightly larger than the total surface to cover. For example, if the size of the cake is 6 inches and 3 inches tall, you double the height (3 inches doubled is 6 inches) then add the diameter of the cake tin (6 inches), which gives you a total diameter of 12 inches.

3- Once we have a circle of the correct size, which is not very thin because it could be break (we will need to stretch it a little more) or not very thick because it would mean having an excess of fondant which afterwards will crease and created slight bulges. Keep fondant thickness around 2-3 mm. Place your hands under the fondant evenly always with your palms off the fondant and drape it over the top of the cake, ensuring that all sides are the same length. Place the palm of your hand on top and 'glue' the fondant by moving your palm around the fondant in a circular motion (never press too much or too hard). Make sure there are no bubbles or creases. Then, continue by passing your hand around the edges. When 'glued', continue working down the sides in small movements all around the cake. I would advise to go all around the sides in little steps (bit by bit). See photos illustrated for more guide.

Check the video tutorial.

4- Once we have the fondant completely pasted, pass the palm of your hand on the whole surface of the cake. Make sure the fondant covers the entire cake then proceed to cut away the excess fondant.

5- For a perfect finish: Polish using the two smoother paddles in each hand with small movements, pressing the fondant just a little bit. The aim of this process is to smooth the surface of the fondant, improving its appearance and obtaining a cake ready to decorate.

(E) Decorating ideas and Pictures tutorial

26

MAKE A SIMPLE EASY SUGAR CRAFT BOW

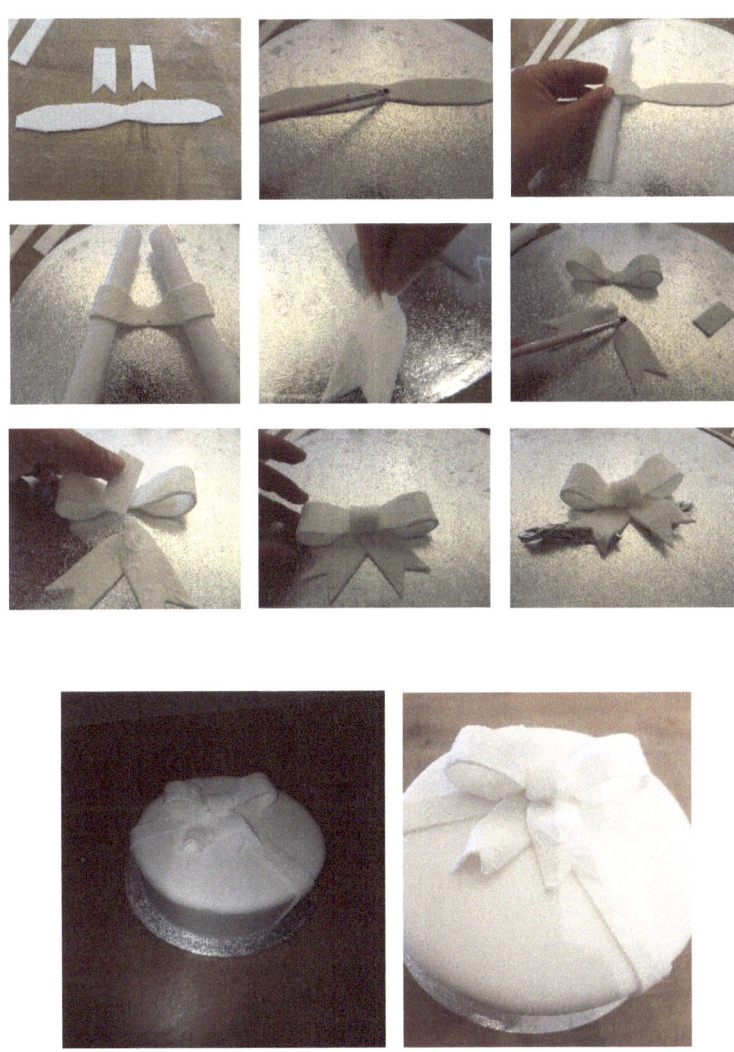

MAKE A SIMPLE EASY SHIRT CAKE

MAKE A SIMPLE EASY TWO TIERS CAKE

1- Cut butterflies and flowers, let them dry for 2/3 days before the cake is done (make different sizes).

2- Add some edible lustre-dusting to the flowers.

3- Bake two tiers cakes (6+8 inches) and allow them to cool to room temperature.

4- Fill the cake and cover a least 2 times with buttercream.

5- Cover the top tier with white fondant (6 inch one).

6- Cut fondant ribbons of approximately 2 cm wide **x** 11cm long (less than 1-inch wide **x** over 4 inches long).

7- With white fondant cover the cake board.

8- Now, on the 8-inch cake (previously covered with buttercream) place the ribbons on the cake as the picture shows.

9- Using a 5-inch cake board to measure, cut a circular shape to remove the excess ribbon on top to the cake. Then cut a circular shape and place it to cover the top.

10- With dark fondant, cut a ribbon and place it on the bottom of the cake (above the cake board)

11- Measure, cut and place cake dowels straws into the cake (or any type of cake dowels).

12- Put some icing sugar on top and place the top tier cake (6 inches white one) and glue it on).

13- Cut a white fondant ribbon and glue it around the top tier cake.

14- Cut a shape in the same colour as the bottom tier and glue some letters in white fondant, then place the shape on the white tier.

15- With icing sugar, glue the flowers all around the cake then the butterflies.

Mistakes that make your cake not perfect and how to solve them

1. The sponge cake has grown irregularly

Sometimes the cakes have an irregular shape, higher in the center and lower in the edges, such as a volcano or hump in the center. This can be due to two reasons:

The dough has an excess of flour: you must check that you have put the correct amount that is indicated in the recipe. If you have done it and it still does not bake as intended to, maybe you should try another recipe (remember that not all the recipes we find in books or on the internet are correct).

The oven's temperature is too high: you should check that your oven is well calibrated or use a furnace thermometer to ensure that the temperature inside the oven is at 180 ° C (or following what the recipe indicates). The temperature must be the same the entire time, from the first second, so always preheat the oven before you start the recipe, to give it time to heat up. Having the temperature too high and then decreasing it (because you forgot to preheat the oven), will be a mistake-resulting in a bad cake.

2. Some area of the cake is burnt

If you have lost track of time and it is past the time of baking, it is normal that the cake is burnt. We cannot do much (except to get you a kitchen timer 😊). But that isn't the case, it can be due to several reasons:

The bottom or sides are burnt. Mold is too large or deep, the mass is more concentrated and the center takes longer to cook. Therefore, by exposing the sponge cake a longer to high temperatures, they may burn slightly. To solve this, you can use a lower and wider mold, or lining the inside of the mold with baking paper, to protect the cake and it not burn it.

The mold is a dark color: although it seems silly, the color of the mold greatly influences the temperature and how it distributes heat. That's why professional molds are usually golden or silver, which absorbs less heat and distributes it better than black molds, which tend to burn the cake. It is also important not to place the mold on a baking tray, which are usually black, but it is preferable to bake it on a rack.

If the mold was touching with other molds or with the wall of the oven, it has been able to receive more heat in the areas that were in contact, which burns the sponge cake. Be careful to always place your molds in the center of the oven.

Burned at the top. The grill was too high: If we put the sponge cake on the top tray in the oven, it is close to the source of heat, it will burn. Ideally, place it a little below the center of the oven. If we see that it is still toasted too much, we can "cover the hearth", or cover it with a sheet of foil or place another oven tray about it to protect it a little from excess heat.

3. The cake has deep cracks

Sometimes, we take a cake out of the oven and find that it has opened or that it has huge cracks on top. This, makes the cake seem very ugly and can result in the cake breaking when unmolding it. It can be due to two factors:

The oven temperature is very high: If we have baked it at a higher temperature, it is possible that the yeast has risen very fast without giving time to form the crumb, which is why the cake has broken. Remember to control the temperature of your oven with an external thermometer to avoid this. The slower the cake is baked, the less likely it is to break into cracks.

We have exceeded the time of baking: If the cake is in the oven longer than what is needed, it can also crack. Be sure to remove the sponge cake the moment it is ready.

4. **The cake center sank**

It is also one of the main problems when baking, it can be due to several reasons.

The temperature of the oven is too low: if the temperature of the oven is lower than that required to cook it, the center of the sponge cake will not cook adequately or develop the crumb when the yeast is raised. That is why this area will be more sunken, and most likely, remain uncooked.

We have opened the oven early: yeast is a rather delicate ingredient, and can play tricks during the baking process. It begins to act at the same moment in which it is exposed to the heat, and like any chemical process, we should not interrupt it. So once the yeast begins to raise the cake, we must keep the temperature of the oven constant until the process is finished, so it is not worth opening the oven, not raise or lower the temperature, or touch anything at all, until at least about 3/4 of the cooking time has passed (at which point the yeast will have finished its part of the work).

Obviously, if you have taken the cake before it has finished cooking, inside it will be half raw and therefore, will not have risen in the center.

The dough has an excess of fat: if the dough has too much fat, it weighs more than normal, and therefore the cake will struggle to rise. Adapt your recipes to have less fat, or replace with a lighter fat, or add a little more yeast to aid in the rising of the cake.

5. The cake is grainy and dry

Have you even bitten into a sponge cake and found that it's dry? Well, if that happens to you, it's because you've done any of these things wrong.

The oven temperature is too low: with a very low baking temperature, the cooking time is increased, which causes a cake that is drier and does not leave the correct texture.

The dough is too beaten: if we go to beat the mixture once we have incorporated the flour, the gluten develops making the proteins are more in proportion. Therefore, more protein, a cake is drier and caked. As a rule, when adding the flour to a mixture, beat the time just to remove the lumps and integrate it, not another second! If it is, you can integrate the flour by hand with a spatula, much better.

The dough has too much flour: if we have gone through the dry ingredients (flour, cocoa, yeast ...) the dough will lack fat or liquid, so it is normal for it to be dry and the texture to not be adequate. Again, be sure to measure the ingredients well, and if you have done it and still do not get good results, remove that recipe from your cookbook and look for a different one.

6. It is too hard on the outside, it has bark

When a cake is too hard, as if it had crust, the first thing we think about is a temperature failure. And indeed, this is usually one of the reasons, but there may also be some more.

The temperature is very high: and yes, my friend, again, the temperature of the oven can be the subject of your headaches ... if it is too high, the cake can become crust, which is the previous step to being burnt.

The dough has little sugar is low fat, or has too much flour: when there is an imbalance in the ingredients, the dough is drier than it should, and it is normal for it to start burning before it would be normal. Therefore, the crust begins to form, which, as we said, is the previous step to being burnt.

The baking time is excessive, and therefore, again the cake is parched and has crust. Some even let the cake cool in the oven when still hot (yes, seriously!), So even if you have turned off the oven, the cake is still baking. Another big mistake!

7. The cake overflows from the mold

Another typical problem is that the cakes rise out of the molds, it overflows on the sides and burns, affecting the result. In that case it does not rise completely, and we do not get a perfect cake. It usually happens for 3 reasons.

Excess yeast: If there is too much yeast in your recipe, the cake will rise more than it should and will overflow from the mold. Be sure to measure the correct amount of ingredients.

The temperature of the oven is very high: if the cake rises too quickly, it can also overflow from the mold, the yeast can make the cake rise more than expected.

We have chosen a mold too small: usually the recipes indicate which mold you should use, but often seeing the dough "by eye" and we think we can put it in a different mold. So, it is best to stick to the instructions and choose the right mold.

* TRICK: If the recipe indicates a larger mold and you do not have it, you can put baking paper on the walls so that it extends a few centimeters above: it is a quick pastry trick to increase the capacity of the mold and the dough does not overflow.

8. The cake is caked

Sometimes the problem is that the cake is left with the crumb too compact, like caked and without holes in the interior. At the time of eating it can become a difficult bite and it is hard to chew. It usually happens for two reasons.

The oven temperature was too low: If the oven temperature is too low, the yeast may not do its work and the dough will not rise. Then we will have a cake with a dense and compact crumb, which has not risen as it should.

We have not beaten the dough well: when it comes to batting the dough, it is very important to introduce air into it, we need to beat very well all the ingredients (especially the egg) to add air to the mixture. The only point where we should not beat too much is after adding the flour, to not develop gluten. But all the ingredients above, need more mixing.

9. The cake does not take golden color

In the case your cake does not take a golden-brown color, it may look too white or what's worse: it may be raw. Here's why this can happen:

The temperature of the oven is not high enough: if the oven does not reach the required temperature, the sponge will stay raw and won't cooked well.

The cake has been covered with aluminum foil / another tray: sometimes we bake several cakes at a time, and another tray or cake may have covered the one that has not baked well. In that case, be sure to rotate them. It may also be that you have put aluminum foil to prevent it from burning, but if you put it too soon, it will not give you time to cook it.

10. The cake has not risen

This is usually one of the most common problems when making cakes and there are many reasons behind this error, so let's analyze them one by one:

The mixture is not well beaten: It is always important to sift the dry ingredients and mix them before adding them to the dough, so that the yeast is distributed correctly throughout the sponge cake. If you have not done so, it may not have been well distributed and the cake will not rise equally for this reason.

The dough has too much flour / low in yeast: Again, the making of a sponge cake is a pure chemical process, and we must be rigorous in measuring ingredients. If your dough has too much flour or little yeast, the biscuit will not rise and will be caked.

The quality of the ingredients is bad: Poor quality ingredients can also spoil our sponge cake. What most affects this are very small eggs, a flour with too much protein, expired yeast, a very heavy fat or a poor-quality butter.

The temperature of the ingredients: it is important that the ingredients that we use for our cakes are always at room temperature. If you have used cold ingredients, they probably have not mixed correctly when making the dough, and in addition to not baking well, the temperature will be too low at the beginning of the baking process, therefore the mixture will stay uncooked and the yeast will not activate- this means the cake does not rise.

11. The cake is stuck to the mold.

If at the time of unmolding the cake you find this nasty surprise, it can be for several reasons.

The mold is not in good condition: it is very important to clean and keep the molds in good condition so that they do not spoil and maintain their non-sticking qualities.

We have not greased it correctly: it may be that we have not greased the mold well, it is best to use melted butter and distribute it well with a silicone brush, and then sprinkle with flour or cocoa (if your cake is chocolate). You can also use a spray release agent. Although the best and most advisable is to line your mold with baking paper, this way you always ensure that the cake does not stick and that the mold stays in good condition.

As you can see, there are a lot of factors to keep in mind, but we can narrow them down to the following points:

Control ingredients: must always be at room temperature, must be of good quality, and must be measured well.

Follow the recipes word by word: to be rigorous in the quantities, in the process of mixing and elaboration.

Know your oven well: make sure the temperature is correct and constant, and know exactly where and how to place your cake to bake.

Control the cake during cooking: the key is to know when it is done, do not open the oven early, and do not leave it too short or too long.

Respect the cooling process: leave the cake a least 20 minutes in the mold, do not cut the baking process.

Practice and little and follow these tips, you will see how you will always get a perfect cake. Keep these general tips in mind and you will see how your cakes change for the better!

I would like to express my greatest gratitude to the people who have helped and supported me throughout the making of my book.

A special thank you goes to RICARDO ALITTA who made the front cover and video explainer.

wrick@hotmail.co.uk

Another special thank you to Marcin Gebler who made this book possible.

As well as a thank you to Maia Gonzalez for proofreading the book.

www.ingramcontent.com/pod-product-compliance
Lightning Source LLC
Chambersburg PA
CBHW041725070526
44586CB00001B/8